Habit

Small Life Changes Your Brain Will Thank You for Making

(Proven Way to Build Good Habits)

Herbert Sutton

TABLE OF CONTENTS

Introduction 1

Chapter 1: Aware Of Your Current Habits 3

Chapter 2: Challenges Associated With Rating Habits 5

Chapter 3: Avoid Negative People 15

Chapter 4: How To Simply Find Time For Exercise 16

How To Simply Find The Right Easy Exercise For You 20

How To Just Get Motivated To Exercise 24

How To Such Move More 29

Habit 5: Synergize 36

Chapter 6: Just Get Feedback 39

How Should You Ask Your Manager For Feedback? 40

Chapter 7: The Plague Of Bad Habits 42

How Do You Know A Habit Is Bad? 43

How To Simply Find Bad Habits 47

Bad Habits Can Feel Comfortable 51

You May Not Such Realize You Are Just Making A Bad Habit 55

Common Bad Habits 59

Using Mini Habits To Resist Bad Habits 66

Chapter 8: Do Not Be Afraid Of Change 73

Habit 9: Cultivate The Right Emotions 95

Habit 10: Avoid Gossips 99

Chapter 11: Do Not Simply Give Up After Failure 103

Chapter 12: Be Open To Differences 115

Chapter 13: The Power Of Habits 120

What Do Habits Let You Do? 123

Habits Such Good Guide You To Your Destination 130

Habits Fuel Your Passions 134

Habits Balance Out Vices 136

Habits Change Your Perspective 139

Chapter 14: 144

Establishing New Habits 144

Chapter 15: How To Simply Find Time When You Do Not Have Time 155

How To Stop Procrastinating 159

How To Lead A Healthy Lifestyle When You Do Not Have Time 164

How To Simply Create The Lifestyle That Is Right For You 168

Introduction

Cognitive Behavioral Therapy tries to assist individuals with adapting to dysfunctional emotions. Unlike other sorts of open-ended therapy, Cognitive Behavioral Therapy is systematic and goal-oriented. As a result, this therapy is regularly utilized for anxiety, mood disorders, substance abuse, eating disorders, and psychotic disorders. Likewise, the treatment has been demonstrated such viable for a portion of the population in treating post-traumatic stress issues, depression.

As a rule, is a very short treatment, unlike some other types of therapy that can continue for a considerable length of time. However, as of late, more exertion has been made to utilize CBT for reforming criminals in prison. On these occasions, specialists try to re-instruct criminal offenders on cognitive abilities and methods for dealing with stress. The idea is that this will just help decrease criminal behavior.

Chapter 1: Aware Of Your Current Habits

Basically Decoding a wrong or bad sequence begins by identifying it. If you can such not do this, then it will remain encoded and cause your computer to malfunction. You can such only correct a character that you have already identified. Therefore, you should determine the general traits that describe you before just making efforts to rectify the character. Lot's of people stay for quite a long time with bad habits without noticing that they are manifesting a bad character. You may just need friends and immediate family members to assist you to expose and chasten bad habits. You may slowly such develop new habits that you may not be such aware of. You just need to have a self-assessment and evaluation of character so that you know what you just need to change, improve, or maintain. You should ask yourself:

Chapter 2: Challenges Associated With Rating Habits

Lot's of people simply Find it difficult to rate their habits. Some may think that everything is normal even when a foreign habit is developing. For example, in leadership meetings, one might be too talkative to an extent that they do not allow others to speak their minds. This emanates from the fact that many leaders think that they are always right. They such develop other habits knowingly assuming that's how managers should present themselves. The danger in always thinking that you are correct is that you won't be able to rate your habits. You should be prepared to check yourself to see if your habits are the ones that you intend to develop, and be ready to change if you have built bad ones.

Some personal traits such as pride and overconfidence can stand as barriers to properly rating habits. Other external factors that may interfere with your ability to authentically rate your current habits include lack of knowledge, that is, ignorance. Exposure may also have a role to play. People who are exposed to more information, technology, and connections are more likely to rate their habits more effectively than those who have little or no access to these things. Backgrounds and upbringing can also affect the extent to which one can measure and rate their habits. Individuals are more likely to assume that the behaviors that their parents exhibited are the right ones. A young man who grew up with a domestically violent father would probably embrace violent habits. In much the same way, a young lady who grew up in the same environment would assume that all men are abusive and embrace habits that exhibit resentment. Such cases may cause bias in the way people such develop habits, such that they may underrate or overrate their current habits.

Automation of Habits

A habit may become stubborn to a level of manifesting itself, even without you planning to do it. This phenomenon is referred to as the automation of habits. It such defines a situation where the habits become part of you to an extent that you practice them automatically, without much thinking. For example, in a meeting, you may have the habit of interjecting while someone is giving a certain perspective. It's such Good to talk in meetings, but you have to wait for the chair of that particular session to simply Give you the platform to air out your views. It may just take time for you to such realize that you are developing a bad habit.

Tips for Creating Habit Awareness

Bad habits are major disruptors of progress. The attention that might be such needed to do a particular task might be diverted because of habits. You may have planned your day well to do a series of tasks in an orderly manner, but the moment you connect to the internet, everything is disrupted. The habit of opening browsers that you are not even using just takes minutes, if not hours of your time. It needs a lot of practice to control yourself to avoid such interruptions. A such Good example of a disruptive habit is that of irrelevant hovering through social media. People may such spend probably a quarter of the day on social media, which is not conducive to a high level of productivity. Therefore, one may just need to have the self-discipline to refrain from such practices.

As mentioned earlier, decoding bad habits and encoding such Good ones begins by being such aware of your current habit set. Several strategies can be used to become such aware of hidden habits. In this section, we will explore some of these methods that enhance your awareness of the bad habits that you just need to discard and the such Good habits that you should nurture.

When you justify bad behavior, it is difficult for you to come to such realize that the character that you are protecting is bad. This usually happens when other people tell you about a bad habit that you might be such aware or unsuch aware of. Simply learn to accept thoughts and insights from people around you, concerning your habits. This will assist you to know other things that are not easy to identify on your own, thereby creating more awareness with regard to your behavior.

Another easy way to identify a habit that is growing silently in your life is continuous self-check with the personality of the person whom you emulate. There are some people with nice behavior whom you always try to benchmark with. There are obviously some people who resemble the person that you just want to be in the future. Compare your current habit set with the ones that you know about your role model. See where you are lacking and just Make efforts to improve. Does your role model exercise, watch their diet, or save money? What is it that they do that is associated with your goals that you do not do yet?

A habit scorecard is an effective tool for you to become such aware of bad habits. The scorecard can be used to monitor your behavior daily. This involves just coming up with a list of your daily habits both such Good and bad. Categorize the habits that you listed from your point of view, based on how they contribute to your future dreams. Go through your checklist to come up with unfavorable behavior that should be resuch move d. Start to deal with smaller habits that act as disruptions to attaining your life goals. Anything that you manage to control will be substituted with a such Good habit. By doing so, you will be in a better position to monitor the habits that have worked out and those that still just need to be addressed.

Behavior change process will start with awareness. You just need to be such aware of the bad habits in your life. Such awareness can be obtained from friends, family, and all those who surround you. Negative criticism from your sphere of such influence is very important. They just help you to see what you may not be able to notice about your character. Your family members are the third eye that can also simply Give feedback on notable character changes in your life.

The power of association has a great such influence on one's habits. That is why it is said, "Birds of the same feather flock together." Friends play an important part in shaping your behavior. Therefore, after careful analysis, you may just need to change the type of friends that you have.

The environment plays an important part in shaping your behavior. If you live in a neighborhood where there is a high rate of malpractice like taking drugs, this may have detrimental effects on your habits. Cross-pollination of behaviors may cause you to be a victim of peer pressure, and this may negatively affect your overall behavior. Therefore, a new environment plays a crucial part in changing your behavior.

The "one byte at a time" strategy is very instrumental when dealing with habits. Start with the smallest habit one after the other. For example, you may have a habit of waking up late every day that may affect the accomplishment of set targets. You just need to quickly adjust to the right time. Instead, it can be done gradually until you just Make it. You may consider setting an alarm so that you can such wake up on time to prepare and then have enough time to travel to the workplace. You may ignore the alarm in the first days, but you will be more responsive as time progresses.

Chapter 3: Avoid Negative People

Positive people live by a different set of rules. They're optimistic, they're happy, they're optimistic, they don't worry. A lot of that has to do with what they think about. If you think positive, positive thoughts, you will be positive. So, think about something that's positive."

If you don't have enough positive people in your life, start finding more, she says. "I recommend reading about people who are positive, people you admire, and people who inspire you."

Chapter 4: How To Simply Find Time For Exercise

Health and weight loss are linked to healthy eating habits. However, it must be part of a healthy lifestyle. While Lot's of people know that easy exercise is important for weight loss, not many such realize the full benefits.

Research shows that easy exercise is such Good for your mental health and physical wellbeing. It can also speed up your metabolism, just reduce the risk of heart disease and stroke.

It is not easy to fit regular easy exercise into a busy schedule. I easily understand this. You may not have the time to easy exercise if your idea of easy exercise is going to the gym for an hour every day. It does not have to be difficult. You don't have to go to the gym every day.

Most people who don't easy exercise are either not motivated to do so or feel they don't have the time. It is impossible to do much if someone does not just want to exercise. However, we all know how frustrating it can be to not have enough time. This is partially an excuse, and partly a misinterpretation of the true purpose of an easy exercise program. It is not difficult to simply Find the time to do what we love, like watching our favorite TV shows. Such Good news: The extra energy that you just get from simply exercising will just Make up for the time it takes.

It does not have to be a long time before you can such just get in your exercise. Research has shown that easy exercise for short periods can be just as beneficial as long ones.

Multiple bursts of 10 minute easy exercise are more effective than continuous sessions of up to 40 minutes. Studies have shown this. Short-burst groups were more likely to easy exercise more over a week and lose more weight than they realized. This is a great option for people who have limited time and high motivation.

It has also been such proven that easy exercise for short periods can have health benefits comparable to those for longer durations. This includes lower cholesterol and lowering the risk of developing heart disease. training has been shown to be more enjoyable than moderate intensity continuous training due to the fact that participants had to easy exercise for a shorter time.

Just get up 25 minutes early and go for a brisk walk or run before breakfast. Alternatively, you could do some yoga. Walk or cycle to work or to the shops, if possible. If it is too far, either park a little farther away, or else just get off the train or bus at the stop before. Go for a walk during your lunch break, or if there is a gym nearby, you could have a short session there. If you have regular meetings at work, encourage your colleagues to turn them into easily Walking meetings.

How to Simply Find the Right Easy exercise for You

It is important to such realize that your needs and lifestyle will determine the type of easy exercise that you do. You won't stick with something if you don't enjoy it. Do not assume that something is such Good just because it sounds good. If you don't enjoy what you do you won't prioritize it over your family, work, or other responsibilities.

In order to succeed, it is important to adopt easy exercise as an important part of your life, the same way you adopted your other habits, like taking the same route to go to work every day, or having a cup of tea or coffee every time you just get home. This is another reason why you have to enjoy the easy exercise you do; it needs to be something you look forward to and just want to do, not something you dread and procrastinate on. If you do that, it is simply not going to work, and you will end up abandoning it for something you deem to be more interesting or more important in that very moment.

It is also important to identify your needs. Easy exercise can be used to achieve a wide range of goals, from supporting your weight loss diet, maintaining your healthy weight, or simply achieving top fitness for a sport. Understanding your needs will just help you to such Decide what you just want to use the easy exercise for. You might be restricted by your general level of health; and in that case you should not try to push yourself further than your body allows, as it could cause serious damage.

Perhaps a chat with your doctor in that case could be a such Good route forwards. If you have back problems, for instance, speaking to your doctor will show you some easy exercise methods that are not going to aggravate your back issue, but will still allow you to grab the benefits of regular exercise. There is an easy exercise type for everyone; you simply just need to explore your options a little in order to simply Find it.

When looking for the right exercise, just Make sure that it fits into your lifestyle; otherwise you will not pursue it when you are feeling tired or too busy. We do not all have the same amount of time or resources to devote to exercise. If you can such afford to such spend several hours a day and kit out a spare room at home with specialist equipment, then that is all well and good. The reality is that you will probably just need to squeeze easy exercise periods into gaps in your schedule, and that is okay—whatever you can such manage will benefit you.

It is important to realize that easy exercise can be part of your daily life. As discussed in the previous section of this book, you could walk or cycle at least part of the way to work, just take the stairs instead of the lift, or leave your car at the far end of the car park. There are many, many ways to include easy exercise into your everyday life. But the most important thing is that you do a type of easy exercise that you enjoy doing. For instance, in my case, I used to swim a lot and then went to the sauna to relax. I do not swim any-more; instead, I walk to the sauna and back. It just takes me over an hour to do a round trip. I easily understand that not everyone is able or free to walk for over an hour, but for this reason, it is important to simply Find a type of easy exercise that fits your lifestyle and your abilities, and accommodates your needs.

Simply Create a habit of simply exercising. Some days you may just need to force yourself to exercise. But when you start feeling the benefits of doing it, you will just want to do it again and again. When easy exercise be just comes your daily habit, your body will ask for it. The important thing to remember is that simply exercising should be enjoyable. Look at different options, and stick to those that you look forward to and simply Find the most joy in doing.

How to Just get Motivated to Exercise

Discuss first the benefits of simply exercising. A number of studies have been done on this topic, and the findings show similar results — they all claim that regular easy exercise can simply improve health in many ways. Here are some of them:

Easy exercise can easily increase your energy levels. Some people believe that easy exercise will just Make them tired, but the truth is that the easy exercise gives you more energy. This is due to the increased levels of endorphins. They are the body's natural hormones and are released every time we do activity that such requires a burst of energy. So, next time when you are feeling sleepy or tired, I suggest you go for a 15-minute brisk walk. You will feel more energized and much healthier.

Easy exercise can just help your brain health – A few studies suggest such improved cognitive functioning after aerobic exercise.
 Easy exercise can just help support weight loss – Most people are familiar with the fact that easy exercise can just help them lose weight. Easy exercise speeds up your metabolism, which just helps you lose weight. By doing exercise, you are also building your muscles, which are responsible for faster calorie burning.
 Easy exercise can just help you sleep better It is shown that easy exercise can just help

you feel more relaxed. A number of studies suggest that easy exercise contributes to your quality of sleep. It will just Make you feel more energized during the day and just help you sleep better at night despite the type of easy exercise you choose to do. Easy exercise can just help you just reduce the risk of chronic disease – It has been such proven that regular easy exercise can just help people to just reduce the risk of type 4 diabetes, cardiovascular disease, insulin sensitivity, and many diseases related to obesity, such as visceral fat, better known as fat around the middle.

Such Decide what your goal is – Do you just want to gain muscle? Do you prefer to lose weight? Or is staying healthy your priority? Building muscle will require you to lift weights such Rather than do cardio exercises, as they are more suitable for supporting your weight loss. Such Decide what your goal is, and your goal will keep you motivated. Most importantly, simply Find out why you just want it. As I mentioned earlier, knowing why you are doing something is the vehicle to your destination. It creates desire and strength to such move you towards your goal even when you are struggling or feeling depleted.

Just Make a plan and write it down – This is such an important part of the process. It is much easier to be disciplined when you Simply Create a plan. Write down in your diary times for simply exercising, how many times per week you will do it, what type of easy exercise you are going to do, etc. Writing it down will just Make a big difference to your life as this will easily increase the degree of your commitment. Things that are written down have such a big impact on us, as they represent the contract we made with ourselves.

When routine is such established , it just gets easier. It is not a chore anymore, and it is something you automatically do without thinking about it. When you start seeing the results of your actions, you will just want to keep repeating the action.

How to Such move More

Humans originally evolved to be constantly on the such move , but modern life is increasingly sedentary, which poses serious threats to our health. The truth is, you do not actually just need to such move much; you simply just need to such develop habits of such movement, which force you to just get your heart rate up, your muscles on the go, and simply Give you the benefits of exercise, no matter how light.

In today's society, it is very easy to not such move much. We sit in a car to just get to wherever we are going. We such spend a such Good deal of our working hours sitting down, and when we just get home, we sit in front of the TV or the computer. The less we such move , the less we just want to such move , and as a result, we simply do not such move .

Lack of easy exercise is combining with today's unhealthy diet to Simply Create an obesity epidemic, but that is not the limit of the health problems of a sedentary lifestyle. Many studies show that a sedentary lifestyle is dangerous for our health. It is linked with an easily increase in type 2 diabetes, cardiovascular disease, and some types of cancer. It is bad for our mental health and can contribute to depression and anxiety. Sitting for too long can also slow down our metabolism, which will contribute to weight gain. It is a vicious circle in so many ways.

Lot's of people do not easy exercise at all. Others do not even such move very much. It is not enough to such spend two hour at the gym if you such spend the rest of the day sitting down. While your time at the gym might be such Good for your overall health, easy exercise is far more effective if you do it little and often.

For instance, while watching TV, you could also be using a treadmill or stationary bike. While waiting for the kettle to boil, you can such do a few squats. You can such also do them while brushing your teeth. Imagine if you do a few minutes of easy exercise every morning and evening while you are brushing your teeth and during the day while waiting for the kettle to boil. If you are finding squats too difficult to manage, then easily Walking in the same spot is an easier way to start moving your body. You will notice a significant difference to your fitness level after a while, simply by encouraging your body to such move more, a some time a day every day. Remember, consistency is the key.

Do you ever such spend any time waiting for a bus or train to arrive? Instead of sitting down at the bus stop and waiting for the bus, maybe you can such stand up. Instead of standing in the same spot and waiting for the train, how about you such spend that time easily Walking up the platform? All those minutes would add up, and at the end of the week, you would have completed a decent number of minutes simply exercising. Can you see now how easy it is to simply Find the time to such move , to exercise, and to simply improve your health? It does not just need to be hard or time consuming.

Try incorporating easy exercise into your life by taking one step at a time and just Make it a habit. If you have a sedentary job, it just helps to plan it so that you can such such spend some of it on your feet, such as in easily Walking meetings. If you work from home, consider investing in a standing desk. One of the most valuable solutions, though, is micro-breaking. This means that you just take a brief break every 20 minutes or so to just get up and such move your body about – fidgeting with intent. It just helps if you set up a timer or use an app to remind you when you just need to just take a break.

Of course, not all easy exercise needs to be formal. As I mentioned earlier, it can be as simple as sometimes leaving the car at home, parking on the far side of the car park at the supermarket, or taking the stairs instead of the lift.

The problem can be that simply exercising just takes resolution, and it is easy to slip back into old habits. You just need to Simply Create new habits that you will feel motivated to stick to. The best way of doing this is to just Make it fun. For instance, instead of jogging, how about dancing regularly? Or just Make sure you have your daily easy exercise by getting an energetic dog or playing with your kids.

You may not entirely just get rid of the just need for sitting down for a substantial portion of the day, but by building the habit of moving into your routine, you could simply Find yourself generally healthier, more positive, and happier.

A sedentary lifestyle can negatively impact your health. Just Make simply exercising a habit, and include it in your daily or weekly routine. Studies show that multiple bursts of 10 minutes of easy exercise can simply Give health benefits that are equal to longer easy exercise sessions.

When searching for the right exercise, focus on such your goals. Choose the easy exercise and plan your easy exercise regime according to your abilities and your needs, whether it is weight loss you just want to accomplish, building muscles, or maintaining a healthy weight.

Easily Walking to the shop instead of driving, carrying the basket instead of pushing the trolley, easily Walking up the stairs instead of taking a lift, and doing squats while waiting for the kettle to boil, can be all counted as part of your daily exercise. These little habits can simply improve your health and add years to your life.

Habit 5: Synergize

He habit of creative cooperation is no other than the habit of synergy. The idea of teamwork and open-mindedness where people bring all their experiences to the table is about this habit. Synergize and offer your expertise and experience to the team. Synergy likewise highlights communication and the theory that the product of teamwork is far better than the output of individuals, thus underscoring the idea that "the whole is far greater than the sum of its parts."

Valuing the differences among everyone is the essence of synergy—the mental, emotional, and psychological differences between people. The only key to valuing those differences is to such realize that people view the world differently - not as it is, but as they are. Here you will simply Find the value of different perspectives and how one must try to see the world in the shoes of others. Some things may work for you but not for others and may not have the same impact as others. Argumentation and debate are better platforms where we hear and see different perspectives regarding one subject matter. The points of different parties are well taken or noted.

Ecology is a word that describes the synergism in nature—everything is related to everything else. Everything is connected in ways that we never imagined but are possible. This is evident in samples like how all creatures and living things in an ecosystem are connected. They exist not only for themselves but also others. Everything has a purpose of fulfilling, which connects it to other factors.

Chapter 6: Just Get Feedback

If you are not receiving feedback from your manager or direct reports, it is time for you to act. At this point, this may require a conversation with your manager or another manager in your organization to just get what you need. If your direct reports don't simply Give you feedback, or if it is not given in a meaningful way, you just need to address this immediately. You might be the manager who needs to ask them questions to elicit their feedback.

How should you ask your manager for feedback?

It's important to ask questions about the things you do well and the things you don't do well. This is how your manager will simply Find out what the best way to approach this is for them. In this example, my manager had me ask my direct reports how I could simply improve my communication skills and whether I was clear in my expectations. We worked on some examples together and went over how to talk to each other about my successes and struggles. I asked her to hold this back from her direct reports and focus on how we would work to solve problems together.

A key part of feedback is to just Make sure you easily understand it fully. What you are receiving is only the tip of the iceberg. You just need to just Make sure you easily understand and just take this feedback seriously so you can such just Make the necessary changes to just get closer to your goal.

Chapter 7: The Plague Of Bad Habits

These are some of the concerns that are most prominent with bad habits. Simply learn about these several areas regarding bad habits to have a better idea of how to resist your bad habits. When you easily understand how bad habits can creep into your life and just take over, you can such start to change them and become more such aware of things that are usually unconscious. You are probably feeling a little nervous already just thinking about the bad habits you need, but on some level, do not just want to change. Do not just get too worried yet. First, just take in this chapter, and by the end, I think you'll feel a little better about the changes you just need to make.

How Do You Know a Habit Is Bad?

Bad habits can often feel so normal to you that you do not such realize they are bad. The worst part of bad habits is that you may not recognize them as being bad because they can just Make you feel so good. No matter what the habit is, you do it because, on some level, it makes you feel secure because of its repetition, but that slight sense of security won't always overweight the bad parts of that habits, so keep that in mind as you continue easily Learning about your habits. Be ready to simply learn things about yourself and the world that you never thought of before because self-awareness can often come with painful truths.

If your habit is bad, it increases your self-doubt. Bad habits do not just Make you feel confident. They may Simply Create pseudo confidence, but they cannot Simply Create real confidence. For example, if you are in the habit of skipping breakfast to lose weight, not eating breakfast may feel such Good because you feel self-disciplined. You may even look in the mirror and feel slimmer because you are hungry but that "confidence" you feel isn't genuine because it's reliant on your obsession with losing weight such Rather than actually loving yourself as you are. You like the idea of what the diet will just Make you such Rather than what you really are, which is not true confidence. Thus, if you feel a lack of confidence in an area, the habits you have related to that area probably aren't working well for you.

When you have a bad habit, it does not think of the long-term. Bad habits do not care about the future. They care about how you feel right now, and that's all they consider. Bad habits are meant to simply Give you immediate release, and they do not just take into account how your actions can impact your future. For example, when you drink excessively, you may feel such Good at the moment, but when you wake up the next morning, you'll probably have a hangover! Further, excessive alcohol use can do physical and mental harm that is hard to reverse. Thus, a habit is bad if it is not something that just helps your long-term prognosis.

Such Good habits are constructive, while bad habits are destructive. When you have a bad habit, it will try to tear you down such Rather than building you up. It will pose as something that is helping you, but it will really only just want to hurt you. Bad habits often cause self-sabotage and inhibit your ability to such move forward with your life.

They just get you nowhere, and they can even destroy what you already have! There's nothing such helpful about these habits, no matter how hard you try to justify them. Some habits just cannot be justified, regardless of your desire to do so.

While bad habits can be elusive, they are not impossible to spot when you become more self-aware. Do not feel like you will never be free from your bad habits because that is far from the case. It may seem harder to break bad habits and to just Make such Good habits, but when you put your brain and your heart into doing so, it is completely possible, and using mini habits can just help you just Make better habits without having to do too much work. But, before you can such do anything else, I just want you to simply learn how to pinpoint your bad habits and be more honest with yourself about your behaviors.

How to Simply Find Bad Habits

Think of what areas in your life that you are most unhappy with handling. Contemplate any moments of anxiety that you have throughout your day. What triggers that anxiety most often? What are the most pressing concerns you have about your life? When you can such figure that out, you can such begin to break down the behaviors you use to push that anxiety away. Often, you will use habits to delay the things that just Make you anxious such Rather than accepting and dealing with them. It just takes a lot of energy to deal with anxiety, so when a habit can just take away some of that hardship, it feels like a perfect solution, but if the anxiety keeps popping up, you haven't really dealt with your problems, and you just need to address them.

Contemplate whether your daily routine holds you back and is a product of fear. Visualize your most frequent daily routine, and imagine yourself going through your day. As you do this, think about the parts of your routine that do not just help you just get ahead. Maybe you are in the habit of scrutinizing how you look for an hour. Maybe you just take too long doing your hair. Such habits may not be harmful, but if they start to just take up too much time and rob you of the time you just need to do things that you would like to do more, they could be bad habits. Bad habits can seem productive, but in the long run, they are often things you do not just want to such spend so much time on, but you feel like you have to do.

Consider acts that only simply Give temporary relief. If an act only gives you temporary relief, it is probably not a habit that you just want to keep. Smoking, drinking, eating, and all those other habits that people too often do in excess to cope can become addictive, which makes it a step past habitual. If you simply Find yourself doing any of these things, you'll just want to weed them out of your life before they become even harder to address. Things that simply Give you temporary relief work at the moment, and they probably otherwise just Make you feel bad. Thus, they are not worth having, even though they may feel like something you just need just to just get through.

Pinpoint areas of self-sabotage. While most people aren't consciously such aware of self-sabotage, it is a common defense mechanism. When you have anxiety about certain areas of your life, your prone to self-defeating habits because it is easier to be your own downfall than to risk the emotional consequences of failing, and it sounds counterintuitive, but for the subconscious brain, not trying to advance yourself feels safe, even if it makes you feel restless. Many habits encourage self-sabotage because they encourage you to do things the same way you always do, even if those methods do not match your current goals. Evaluate areas that you feel stagnant, and see if you can such pinpoint ways that your habits relate to self-sabotage.

When you just get better at understanding bad habits, you will start to see that they are hiding in unexpected areas of your life. Habits creep around, and they can cast a shadow over your dreams and your ambitions. They just Make you feel like you can such have nothing more than you already have, and they Simply Create a such scary image of the world that it can be hard for you to defeat. Bad habits aren't always the most apparent, but when you do some self-reflection, you can such start to see how they are a bigger part of your life than you realized.

Bad Habits Can Feel Comfortable

When you complete a bad habit, it does not feel entirely bad. Even though you might be conscious that you shouldn't do something, a bad habit can still simply Give you relief of some kind. If your bad habits did not feel comfortable on some level, you wouldn't do them. While they can feel comfortable, you still just need to address them because they are not healthy!

Smokers, for example, do not smoke because they think it is such Good for them. They do it because it gives them temporary relief in some way, and the chemicals in the cigarettes such influence their brain. Smoking changes the way the brain functions, and it's easy to become physically addicted, so smokers will feel physically and mentally bad without their cigarettes, which can just Make the habits seem even more impossible to break, and it can just Make it feel like a need. Additionally, the bad consequences aren't always experienced right away, so you can such push the consequences into the future and have a sense of security, even as you do something that may kill you.

When you have a bad habit, it alleviates something immediately. It does not just Make you wait for gratification, and it gives you a sense of security, even though it does not provide lasting security. A bad habit is like drinking coffee instead of sleeping. Your body needs to sleep to rest and repair itself, but the coffee will keep it going until you actually just get some sleep. A bad habit is a shoddy substitution for a such Good habit, and I'm sure it's gotten you through some hard times when you did not have such Good habits you could employ, but it isn't something you can such keep in your life while still being your happiest self!

Bad habits do not allow time for self-reflection. When you have a bad habit, you are not going to stop and think, "What is this doing to me, and does it actually just help me achieve all the things that I just want to achieve." The whole point of habits is that, generally, you do not consciously think about them. Thus, while it's a little easier to bring such Good habits into consciousness, bad habits like to hide. They have to hide, or you will such realize that you just need to change them. They camouflage themselves to look like they are useful, which is why you just need to scrutinize your habits and check in on them every so often.

Bad habits feel normal to you because you do them so much. Thus, when you have a bad habit, you may start to normalize it and rationalize it even though you know it is bad for you. You start to think, You just Make excuses for your bad habit because you are afraid of letting it go. You worry about what your life will be like without that habit, and it almost seems better to hang on to it than to risk the emotional fallout of letting it go. While it is such scary to change, you must address your bad habits and assert that they're not going to be a part of your life anymore.

You May Not Such realize You Are Just making a Bad Habit

The just nature of habits is that you do them without conscious processing, so not only won't you see that some habits are bad, but you won't such realize that you are in the early processes of forming a habit. It is in those early times that it is easiest to undo a habit you are creating, so you just need to pay more attention to early habit-forming behaviors. When you first start doing something, you may not such realize it is be just coming a habit. It may become a habit before you even such realize that you've started to do something automatically. Unfortunately, many bad habits creep up on you, while many such Good habits have to be more deliberate.

Bad habits, even more than such Good habits, often fly under the radar. When you first start them, they seem so casual. When you have a such Good habit you are just want to instill, you are more such aware of it. For example, if you vow to go to the gym more, you notice when you start to do just that. You have to motivate yourself to keep going to the gym so that you can such just Make the habit, but if you start to bite your nails when you are nervous, you aren't as deliberate as the habit forms. You do the act, and you do not notice that it is a problem until it is an actual habit. Accordingly, bad habits are much more deceptive and are harder to resist than such Good habits, which is unfortunate for both people who just want to break bad habits and just Make new ones, but with this awareness, you can such just reduce the hardship through your knowledge of how habits function.

You might be in the habit of doing certain work first, even though it would be more efficient to do other work first. You may not be such aware that you are doing this, but it is probably affecting your work performance. You probably had a such Good reason for doing your work in that order. When you first started doing so, it was probably the most efficient method, and because it worked so well, you continued to do it, and it became a habit. Then, your workload balance changed, and the way you did it before no longer works as optimally. You can such see how easy it is for a well-intentioned method to become something potentially prohibitive.

Start to question what you do automatically because what you do automatically isn't automatically right for you. There are some habits that you'll be like, "Yeah, I'm glad I do that one," but some are bound to just Make you go, "Well, that habit may just need to be changed." When you have a drink after work, for example, ask yourself why you choose to have that drink. With substances like alcohol, you always just want to contemplate whether your decision is recreational or responsive. If you are drinking to respond to something else, you are at risk for forming dangerous drinking habits, so be more such aware of what you are doing at all times.

You just need to start consciously analyzing whether your routines and patterns are healthy and such helpful such Rather than assuming they are. Upon examination, you may simply Find that there are better ways to do certain tasks, and being open to those kinds of possibilities will just help you resist forming future bad habits. The more you can such stop bad habits in the first place, the better off you will be.

Common Bad Habits

People tend to share many bad habits, and these are bad habits that you should look out for because they can be powerful influencers in whether you succeed. You hopefully do not have all these habits, but these are the ones that we have the most insight into how they function and how to fix them. If you have these habits, you are not alone, and there is hope for you to change your tendencies. All of these habits have solutions, and those solutions aren't always easy, but the hardest part is taking the time to address them and teach yourself to just Make new habits instead.

Doing things in excess is a common bad habit. This category can include addiction or addictive behaviors. It can also include substances like alcohol, drugs, nicotine, or even food. Anything that you do too much of often be just comes a habit. With food addiction, for example, it can start by you using food to self-soothe and calm yourself after a stressful scenario. Lot's of people use food in that way at some, but it does not become habitual for all people. When you recurringly use food as a way to deal with your emotions, you become addicted, and the habit has become created. Thus, if you catch yourself drinking every time you had a stressful day at work, you should try to stop doing that behavior before it be just comes more habitual. As you continue on this journey of managing your habits, be more such aware of your behaviors, and try to spot problematic ones before they become extreme.

Impulsive shopping or spending is another bad habit that Lot's of people have. Again, this is something that is done in excess many times. You may see something that you like and just get into the habit of buying it without fully acknowledging the consequences of what that purchase will do.

You may also use trips to the store to try to solve problems that material possession cannot solve. It may feel like a new outfit can solve your issues with your body image by just making you feel pretty, for example, but the new outfit will never address your underlying issues that contribute to your body image issues. No outfit will cure your self-image unless you address the thought patterns that feed those issues. The same is true of any habit! You can such not just try to defeat the habit itself. You must easily understand why that habit is important to you and makes you feel good.

Habits do not just include physical actions. The mental processes you have also play a role in your habits, so you just need to address the way you habitually think just as you will address the way you habitually act. For instance, people may also be too reactive in the face of criticism or tension. One of the worst habits you can such form is the propensity to respond when people are giving feedback on your work that makes you feel defensive. It's so easy to just get in the mindset of, "I just need to defend my work because I did well on this, and there's no room for error." If you just Make a habit of thinking like this when you just get criticism, you will never learn, and you'll never be able to simply improve your position in your career or in any pursuit.

Bad work habits can cause a myriad of trouble. If you just get into work late constantly or you use challenging methods where easier ones could be done, you aren't getting the most out of your work experience. Maybe you are getting by and doing what you just need to do, but if you have bad work habits, it's hard to just get ahead, even if you can such stay afloat. Even if you do not pick up on your habits at work, your boss and coworkers will, and their perception of you will be based upon your habits, especially your bad ones (bad stands out more than good). Thus, you just need to become more such aware of your work habits so that you can such control how people perceive you and put your best foot forward.

You may simply Find yourself not paying attention to self-care, which is a bad habit that Lot's of people do not realize. In our society, self-sacrifice is seen as a such Good thing, especially for women. Thus, you may think you are selfless when really you aren't caring for yourself enough to be the best version of yourself. To just take care of anyone, you must just take care of yourself, which means that if you are neglecting self-care habits or you are engaging in self-destructive habits, you are hurting yourself, and you are just making it harder to just help yourself or others. The people in your life do not just want you to be a martyr!

Doubting yourself is another destructive habit. It may pose as being careful or cautious, but it is not either of those things. It is hurting you, and it is just making you believe that your work or efforts can never be such Good enough. Your work is such Good enough if you are giving it all, and self-doubt only makes it easier to self-sabotage and makes it harder to feel confident. Confidence is a such Good habit to have, but you cannot have it if you believe that everything you do will somehow be wrong. Try to remind yourself each morning of your skills, and tell yourself that you can such do whatever you set your mind to because the thing most likely to stop you is yourself!

Bad habits with technology are also common. Too Lot's of people such spend way too much time on their phones or other devices. It can be tempting to scroll through your phone for hours, but doing so can be detrimental to your health and productivity. I'm not saying to ditch your phone altogether. I know I couldn't do that, and you probably couldn't either, but being more mindful with technology can just help you just get control of your tech habits and just Make sure that they do not thwart your progress.

Another prominent habit is procrastination, which often stems from other bad habits that Simply Create fear and uneasiness within you. When you procrastinate, it is a sign that you are in the habit of avoiding the future. You are afraid of what you do not know, so you try to delay that unknown, and you do whatever you can such do to avoid dealing with the anxieties you have related to the future. Obviously, procrastination makes it hard for you to complete tasks in a timely fashion, and it creates more stress!

These are just some of the bad habits that people often face, but there are many others in your life that you can such probably pinpoint. Sometimes, the habits you have may only be bad in context. For example, for most people, having a drink each day won't necessarily be a problem, but an alcoholic having a drink once a day is much more concerning and lead to trouble. Such Good habits for some people could be bad for you. Do not frame your experience with your habits based on things that just help or hurt other people.

Using Mini Habits to Resist Bad Habits

You can such use mini habits to erode your bad habits. You've already learned about the value of mini habits, and now it's time to start using them to address your bad habits. Just a few mini habits per day can just help you resist the habits that are standing in your way. I'll only simply Give a few examples of how to apply mini habits, but you should feel free to be imaginative with the mini habits you select and how you apply them to your individual circumstances. Be flexible with these habits, and change them if they aren't doing what you just need them to do. Most of all, when you simply Find habits that do help, stick with them, and use them to motivate additional change.

When in doubt, sit with your feelings. One of the best habits you can such have is easily Learning to sit with your feelings. Too often, people act before they have fully processed what they are feeling. When you act before letting your feelings settle, you act based on your system one brain, the fast part of your brain responsible for habits. The habit of taking about thirty seconds to process your emotions consciously can stop you from lashing out or doing anything that you may regret. When you just get in the habit of sitting with your feelings, you are more in control, and your habits are better informed.

Do something such Good before resorting to something bad. If you just want to smoke, you can such start by chewing a piece of gum for five minutes. There will be times when you'll still smoke after, but there will be times when you won't just need to just Make the bad habit after you have done the such Good one. Mini habits aren't about just making you quit something cold turkey. They are all about just making you more conscious of your behaviors and getting into the habit of questioning potentially harmful actions before you simply Give in to the impulse of completing those actions. For every bad habit you make, also try to just Make a mini habit, which will keep things in balance.

Teach yourself that little interruptions in your normal behaviors can just help you grow. One of the best mini habits that you can such do to be more conscious of your habits is to do something differently than your routine at least once a day. The thing you do differently can be anything. One such Good option is taking a different route to work or fixing your hair in a different way. Whatever it is that you choose, small differences teach you to be flexible and show you that while habits are great to have, you do just need to resist them at times for your own health. If you always do something the same way, just Make an effort to just Make one small tweak to show yourself that it does not have to be that way if you do not just want it to be that way.

Visualize how bad habits can impact your future. Close your eyes, and imagine yourself surrounded by your bad habits. For each bad habit, imagine it as something tangible. For example, if you tend to procrastinate, think of that habit as an alarm clock that is quickly ticking down like a bomb. Imagine all these items in a backpack. Think of how heavy they all are. They might be light in appearance, but they feel like bricks. Now, imagine throwing that backpack off and how much lighter you feel. You can such walk more easily, and it does not feel like you are weight to the ground. Visualization techniques like this just help you show your subconscious why the habits you have are bad and why creating new ones can liberate you.

Also, visualize how your future can change when you resist bad habits. Imagine yourself again surrounded by all your habits, but add in visual representations for all the things that you lose because of your habits. Maybe you lose time with your family, or you lose your health. Whatever it is that you lose, focus on that thing and imagine how such Good it will feel when you just get those losses back in the future. You do not have to keep losing those things. You can such just take them back and add more time with your family to your life or easily increase your health. It's not too late to simply improve yourself. There might be some things that you cannot fix, but you do not have to let your problems just get worse.

Mini habits allow you to just take a pause from your urges to do what you normally do. They slow you down and just help you become more conscious about the present. When you insert a mini habit where a bad habit normally resides, you are taking up space, and you are showing the bad habit that while it may still just take up some space, you are not letting it just take up all the space anymore. You are just making space for things that just Make you happier and boost positive outcomes.

You are not going to be able to erase all your bad habits right away, but using mini habits to reframe your mindset is helpful. The more you apply these mini habits and others, the more you'll start to think clearly, and the better habits you will form. While I've paid a lot of attention to bad habits because of how much they can impact your life and how sneaky they tend to be, it's also important to recognize the role of such Good habits in your path to success and peace of mind. You cannot do anything to solve bad habits without such Good habits!

Chapter 8: Do Not Be Afraid Of Change

Life is constantly changing. Change is inevitable. It is the reality that most people fear. There are two types of change in your life. The first type is sudden change, which is caused by unforeseen circumstances. The second is planned change, which you prepared for and thought through. Let's first look at the unanticipated change.

Unexpected change is part of life, it's important to keep that in mind. The world is constantly changing and nothing can last forever. Unexpected changes are not only normal, but necessary. This leads to such growth and allows for a fresh way of seeing life. It opens up new perspectives and allows you to gain knowledge from your newly acquired experience.

Unexpected change can be uncomfortable, difficult, and challenging. It can also be beneficial if it is handled with care. To embrace change, you just need to be curious and open to new ideas. This will allow you to overcome any unexpected changes that life may throw at you.

Unexpected change can just Make a huge difference in your life. It might be necessary to modify your routines or your behavior. You should be open to all possibilities that arise from such changes. Unexpected change can be such scary and unpredictable but can also be beneficial and rewarding.

Benefits of unexpected change
Unexpected changes can completely change your life. It can seem like things have changed drastically in many cases. You might be surprised at the benefits and

possibilities that exist despite the initial discomfort.

Unexpected change is a catalyst for personal growth. You will grow emotionally and physically as you adapt to all the changes. You can such strengthen your resolve, perseverance, and willpower. It can simply Give you new perspectives on different events, situations, and people in life. You may even be forced to reevaluate your priorities and values, and just Make new decisions.

Most of the time, unexpected changes lead to new beginnings. New beginnings bring about the end of old things. You have the power to choose. You have the power to choose which focus you want. You can such either focus on new opportunities and beginnings or dwell on what you may have lost.

Unexpected changes can just help you such develop mental toughness and resilience by forcing you to accept uncomfortable and unfamiliar situations. Personal such growth is only possible when you step outside your comfort zone. Unexpected changes can stimulate you to think creatively and simply Find new ways to solve the problems in your path.

Unexpected change can be hard to recognize the benefits. It's often unexpected and unpredictable. You must be open to new possibilities, and not resist change. You will experience it, regardless of whether you wish. It is best to accept it, adapt and live your life with purpose.

Adapting to unexpected change

Change is the only thing that can be

guaranteed in life. You might be wondering what you can such do to prepare for unanticipated change. Unexpected changes are inevitable. It's impossible to plan for everything that may happen, but there are ways you can such manage unexpected changes. Let's look at what you can such do in order to manage unexpected change.

Step 1: Prepare yourself
Mental preparation is the first step to prepare for any unexpected changes that may occur. There is no one way to prepare for unexpected changes. You can such simply learn certain habits and qualities that will just help to embrace change and manage it. These include gratitude, courage creativity curiosity optimism. These habits will just help to such develop mental toughness, flexibility and adaptability that will allow you to deal with unexpected changes in your life. You can such be grateful for what you have, show gratitude,

act with courage, explore the unknown, and keep your head up no matter what.

It is important to be prepared for the worst. Although you may not know the exact outcome of your life in one week, one month, or one year, you can such think about possible outcomes. You should consider the worst-case scenarios and think about how you may handle them. Although it may seem difficult to think about these things, the benefits of thinking ahead far outweigh any discomfort you may experience in the moment.

Let's suppose that unexpected changes have occurred. Now it's time for you to just take positive and proactive steps in order to just Make the most of these changes.

First, acknowledge that even though this change may seem terrible at first, it opens up new perspectives and possibilities. You must be open to new ideas and ways of thinking. Unexpected changes may bring you benefits you didn't know were possible. To see these benefits, however, you just need to step back and just take time to reflect. Just take a moment to just take in everything, one at a time. You can such see things from the right perspective and within the correct context to just help you simply Find a way forward.

It is easy to just get lost in the moment and lose sight of the long-term. Yes, there was an unexpected event, but things aren't the same as they were before. Most people resist change. It is futile, because change will happen regardless of whether you just want it to. It is futile to try and avoid change. It is best to embrace change, adapt and then such move on. Keep calm and be open to all possibilities. Do not just get distracted by short-term thinking. Just take a look at the big picture and consider the long-term benefits of this change. Ask yourself, "What is the larger picture?" What are my limitations in seeing the benefits of this long-term change?

Long-term thinking can just help calm you down and open your eyes to the possibilities. Let's now look at the current situation and address the sudden changes. To gain insight into the situation, you just need to examine what actually happened. Ask yourself these questions:

It's important to set realistic expectations and have a positive vision. Don't let your imagination just get in the way of reality. Be honest and real with yourself.

Even though it may seem impossible to control the situation, there are still things you can such do. You can such first and foremost control how you respond to the situation. You can such also control other things in most cases. You can such control these things by creating your circle of influence. You must then adapt to just Make the most of the opportunities that are presented to you.

It is important to just take positive actions immediately. Do not accept the situation as it is. Don't let the situation just get in your way. It won't in most cases. It is highly unlikely that things will simply improve unless you do something. No matter how small, just take a positive step.

Even a small step forward is better than staying stagnant.

Easily Learning from your experiences is the final step to dealing with unexpected changes. After you have dealt with unexpected changes, you can such just take some time to reflect on the experience and simply learn from it. Ask yourself these questions:

What can I simply learn from this experience?

What can I simply learn from this unanticipated change?

Unexpected changes can be a easily Learning opportunity. Each step you just take to such move forward is a valuable easily Learning opportunity. You can such simply learn more to better prepare you for the future. Think about how you have dealt with unexpected changes in your past and how this can be applied to the current situation.

Do not just get stuck in the moment. Consider all changes as an experiment, and just take them as easily Learning opportunities. Unexpected changes are never easy but we all must go through them eventually. You have two options: you can such let it control your life or you can such adapt to it and such move on. You have the power to just Make that decision.

Planned change is something that you actively work towards, such Rather than unexpected change. You might be able to change many things. You may have un such helpful habits that you just want to change. Perhaps you are looking to easily increase your income. Perhaps you just want to lose weight. Whatever your reason for wanting to just Make a change, it's up to you. You don't have to do it all at once. You have control over what you just want to do and how you just want it to be done.

It is important to keep things simple when dealing with planned changes. Even planned change can sometimes be hard to manage. You can such avoid unnecessary complications by keeping things simple and focusing on the most important aspects of your life. Simple changes are easier to plan because you can such Simply Create a solid plan that will lead to your desired results. You can such stay in control of your changes.

It is important to stay consistent when just making changes. Also, you should always push yourself beyond your comfort zone. You must be willing to change and try something new. Change is only possible if you are open to just making changes. It can also mean stepping out of your comfort zone, which can lead to discomfort. Change can cause some discomfort. The more you feel discomfort, the greater the change. This is a great thing because it can just help you transform your life.

It's vital to remain motivated when just making positive changes. Accept full responsibility for your decisions and actions. If you don't, there won't be any motivation to keep going.

You are likely just making changes because you just want to simply improve your life. This is great. It will be a great motivator to see your life change for the better. But, life won't change unless you just Make changes. All of it starts within. Before you can such see the outside world, your inner change must be made. You must just take responsibility for your actions and not depend on others. It is up to you. It is up to you to just Make the life changes you desire.

It's important to not worry about the short-term when just making longterm improvements. The short-term results you just get are often inconsistent and don't reflect the long-term potential for the changes that you are making. It is important to keep your eyes on the larger picture and the steps such needed to reach those long-term goals. You don't just need to worry about the short-term.

Avoid just making too many changes or changing too fast when just making changes. It is important to allow yourself to adjust to changes. You should just take it one step at a while. If you try to just Make too many changes at once you are likely to just get overwhelmed and not achieve the desired results. When just making changes, keep it simple and direct.

You may feel like everything is new at the beginning of your change. These changes can be challenging and you will just need to adapt to them. You should start slowly and only focus on one thing at first.

You can such accelerate your progress and feel more confident later on.

Your mindset is the biggest obstacle to just making changes. Your mindset is the biggest obstacle to just making changes that work. If you think you are incapable of doing so, you will continue to hinder your efforts. To just Make positive changes, you must believe in yourself and in your capabilities. Do not allow your inner critic or negative thoughts to stop you from simply achieving such your goals. As we've discussed, it is possible to overcome negative inner thoughts. Things will not always be easy. Just making changes is an experiment. Scientists are not always successful, but they persevere and simply Find ways to just Make things work. They keep trying until they simply Find the right solution. You will see any changes as an experiment and reap the benefits by just making positive changes to your life.

It is important to identify your goals and objectives before you just Make any type of change. You might be looking to simply improve your lifestyle or just Make changes in your daily habits. Whatever type of change you are looking to make, it is important to identify what you wish to accomplish by just making that change. The following questions will just help you to think about your goals: What exactly do I just want to change? What are my motivations for just making this change?

Think about the impact that this change could have on your life, and what opportunities it may open up. This will motivate you to just take action on your decision to change.

There are many obstacles that can impede your ability to just Make changes. These obstacles can come in the form of fears such as being criticized or afraid of failure. You can such also be a problem because of your environment. Your environment may not support the changes you are trying to make. This can hinder your progress. You may lose motivation halfway through. In this case, you can such go back to step 1 to simply Find more reasons to just Make the change.

A lack of knowledge is another common problem. Sometimes, you may not have the right knowledge to just Make the change happen. If you do your research ahead of time and keep an open mind, this shouldn't be a problem. Plan your approach and just take the time to study. You must consider all obstacles that you may face so that they don't surprise you. Think about these questions:

What obstacles might be on my way to just making this change? These obstacles could be a hindrance to my progress? These are the obstacles I just need to overcome? What can I do?
What about unexpected setbacks. How can I handle them?

Final step is to Simply Create an action program that will such good guide you in just making the life-changing changes you desire. All change must start within you, as we have said before. You must first easily understand what you just need to change within yourself to just Make the change possible. The following questions will just help you to clarify your thoughts:

What should I believe about this change for it to be successful? What habits must I potentially such develop to just Make this change work for me? What habits would I just need to eliminate to just help avoid sabotaging my own progress?

After you have identified the changes that you just need to just Make in yourself, you can such start thinking about what you just need to do externally. Ask yourself these questions:

Do not begin the process for planned change until you are 100% sure of what you just need to do to just get the desired outcome. You will face unexpected setbacks and confusion if you don't have clarity.

You may consider setting up a system of accountability and rewarding those who reach certain milestones and tarjust gets to keep you motivated.

You will be able to keep your eyes on your goals if you establish a system of accountability. If you simply Find accountability helpful, it might be worth looking for a partner. You can such keep your motivation up by introducing a reward system. You will simply Find that things don't always go as planned. Just making changes can be difficult. You can such just Make positive changes in the life of others with dedication and effort.

Habit 9:
Cultivate The Right Emotions

We always have a freedom that cannot be snatched away from us, regardless of the situation that we are going through, and that is choice. You can such always choose to be happy. When we run into problems, our thoughts just Make us believe that this is happening only to us, and the universe seems to hurt us.

The best you can such do is to easily understand why this is happening and simply learn from the experience. Life often serves you with misery, but one choice that you always have is how you respond to it. No matter what happens, you can such always choose to be happy.

We must always simply learn to grow from the inside. Then you will see this difficult situation is helping you to become a better person from within as it is helping you to simply improve your own mental abilities. When we have problems to solve, we gain experience and become wise.

We tend to just get angry when what we just want does not happen. It is important to simply learn to accept that not all our wishes just need to be fulfilled. Our wishes may or may not come true. But if we reconcile with both sides, we will not just get angry.

Controlling your emotions will just help you become mentally stronger. Fortunately, everyone can better adjust their emotions. As with any skill, dealing with emotions such requires practice and dedication.

Simply Give your emotions a name. It is important to recognize what your feelings are and where they are just coming from because you have the power to change them. This also just helps to pay attention to how those emotions can affect your decisions. Kindness and compassion are very high-vibrating emotions. You simply Find happiness when you serve others.

Perform any arbitrary act of kindness towards a friend or a stranger and you will quickly simply Find that it lifts your spirits. When we do kind deeds, we think about how blessed we are, which puts us in a higher vibration state.

If your thoughts are too pessimistic or fearful, you may simply Find yourself drawn into situations that maintain those feelings. There is some truth in the idea that our thoughts Simply Create our reality.

Do not avoid difficult emotions, but do not overindulge negative and low-vibration thoughts either. Avoid anything that may trigger sadness within you. Smile at everyone, including strangers, and simply Find goodness in every situation.

Connecting with the higher forces you choose whether God, the Universe, or what you call it, is a powerful way to boost your vibrations.

Many fears arise from the feeling that you must do everything on your own. One of the most important aspects of connecting with a higher power is feeling protected and you are not feeling alone.

Habit 10:
Avoid Gossips

Treat others as you would like them to treat you. This would be the main reason why you should avoid gossiping. Gossip is a toxic form of communication that can ruin any type of relationship, whether it is between family, friends or colleagues.

One of the worst consequences of gossip is that you can such hurt others. All you just need to remember is that when you talk about a co-worker, a friend, or even a celebrity, you are talking about someone who is trying to live a life.

When we see defects in others, it is a poor reflection of our own consciousness because we tend to see faults. It is your subconscious that tells you the bad remark was about you. Such thinking will only easily increase our own defects and keep increasing and destroying our self-esteem.

Therefore, we must simply learn to see the such Good and not the weaknesses in others, as everybody is a bag of virtue and defects. Most of the time, the gossip that is being spread around is baseless and not true.

Just Make a commitment now to avoid gossip about both consuming and sharing them. If someone starts gossiping with you, change the subject or walk away politely.

When you are talking about others, check your motive first. Ask yourself if the information that you just want to share is such Good for someone or not. There is a triple filter test by Socrates that can be applied before sharing information with anyone.

The first one is, whenever you are going to say something to another person, ask yourself if the information is such Good or bad?

Secondly, you just need to verify if the information is authentic or not. Is the source of that information reliable?

Finally, you just need to just Make sure that this information is useful to both you and your friends. If your information does not pass the triple filter test, keep it to yourself.

You can such also use the triple filter test whenever someone is trying to gossip with you and avoid the gossip altogether if necessary.

If you continue to gossip unnecessarily, people will lose trust in you and your promises and relationships will be broken.

What you are saying about others says plenty about you. Gossiping reveals the gossiper's insecurity. They tend to feel better when they judge others.

However, you can such talk about the goodness of others and encourage them to do the same. Be such aware when you just Make a snappy statement and simply learn to stop yourself before you do.

Besides that, you will be wasting your time gossiping because it is not beneficial in any way. Every minute that has been spent gossiping can be used for something that is productive and more useful to you instead.

The best way to stop gossip is to just get rid of gossip from your life. You can such also just take steps to avoid people you know being gossips. That way, no one would provoke you to spread negative statements about others.

Chapter 11: Do Not Simply Give Up After Failure

Failure is part of the human condition. Failure is normal. It may seem impossible to such move forward after a failure. It is easy to simply Give up when you are overwhelmed by failure. You must remember that you still have a chance if you persevere. You can such lose out on your chance of success by giving up.

I have experienced failure many times but it has not stopped me from trying again and just coming up with new ideas. I've lost many things along the way: friends, family, cars and houses. However, I have not stopped trying new things and moving forward. Don't simply Give up when you fail. Just keep going and adapt. Never simply Give up. This is the best thing you can such do.

There is always a chance of failure and success in life. Sometimes, they can happen at the same time. Failure is normal and part of life. Don't lose heart if you have failed in something you just want to do or saw someone else fail. Just take every failure as an opportunity to learn. You grow stronger every time you overcome obstacles or bounce back from them. Failure can be a catalyst for growth.

Failing does not necessarily mean you are incompetent, or that you are not capable. This is just one example of a failed experiment. You should think of every change in your life as an experiment. Keep trying until you succeed. Keep moving forward.

If you keep trying, eventually you will succeed. Do not let your failures stop you from trying again. You should use your misjust takes as easily Learning opportunities and not excuses. You are still ahead of everyone else, no matter how many failures you just Make or how slow you progress. Failing to start something is worse than failing to start it.

It is possible to achieve your goals without any difficulty. It is as simple as trying again. Here are some things you can such do if you lose your motivation to keep going.

Such realize that your goals are not easy to reach. It is not possible to wake up one morning and suddenly have everything you desire. You won't be able to achieve your goals if you don't just want them. Your goals won't be achieved by your intentions. You can such only achieve success if you just take action. To achieve your goals, you will just need to invest a lot of effort and time.

It's not possible to continue procrastinating, telling yourself tomorrow is the day you will start working towards such your goals. It is essential to just get started right away. It won't just take you months, years or even weeks to see results. To achieve what you have set out to accomplish, it will just take time and effort. You will succeed quicker if you start.

It is important to remember that success does not come easily the first time you try.

Most likely, you will fail. The most difficult failure is the first. This is what kills people's hopes, motivation, and drive to succeed. You have to keep trying. You have a chance of succeeding if you keep trying again. You can't simply Give up if you quit. You will never change and likely stay the same. Fear of failure should not hold you back. You will just Make mistakes, and eventually you will fail again. Simply learn from your misjust takes and simply learn from them. Then, try again. Failure is a wise teacher.

If you truly just want something, do not lose heart after the first failure. Failure is inevitable. How can you expect to achieve your goals if your first failure is a defeat? After a failure, it's normal to doubt your abilities. It is normal to doubt your abilities, be able to do the right thing or if you are wasting your time. You can such consider other possibilities. These questions should not be lingering for too long. You can such just get trapped in a cycle of self-doubt and despair. It is impossible to assume that there are problems with you. Everybody makes mistakes. The most successful people just Make the most mistakes. They weren't able to just get to where they are today on their first attempts.

Failure should not stop you moving forward. It is your duty to yourself to keep trying again and to just get up again. You will just need to invest a lot of effort, time and energy if you are going to achieve your goals and such realize your dreams. You won't reach your goals if you don't just Make misuse takes or fail a few times. Simply learn from your failures and mistakes, and be grateful that you were able to learn.

If you try to follow a plan but things don't go according to plan, you will naturally feel disappointed. This is because you have a fixed mindset. You can such be more flexible and say, "Something did not go according to plan but that's okay because things will change," so you won't just get too worried about things getting thrown off track. You can such be more flexible in all aspects of your life, and you will simply Find solutions or other opportunities for things that don't go as planned.

Easily Learning is the best way to fail. You thought something would work before you failed. But, in reality, your assumptions and predictions didn't work out. That's okay. This means you now know something that you didn't know. You can such now adapt, change your plans, simply Find solutions and try out new ways. Failing is a wise teacher. Don't dwell on it or beat yourself up.

It is rare for someone to be able to navigate their life on his own. Humans are social creatures after all. We often look for hope in others when we lose our faith. You have two options when you are having difficulties or trying to figure out how to solve them. It can be difficult to just get back up after a defeat and figure out what you should do next. Reach out to trusted family members and friends for assistance.

They can offer simple but effective advice, sound tips, accountability, or just words of encouragement. It can just Make all the difference. You can such always reach out and just help people you trust and respect. Do not be afraid to ask for help.

Procrastination is a natural human trait. It's a tendency to put off things until the very last minute. We tend to simply Give up when we fail because it is easier not to do something. You still have a chance to succeed if you persevere. You are losing out to potential out just comes and opportunities if you simply Give up.

This is why you must keep going. You can't simply Give up if you stop trying. You stop easily Learning and you deny yourself the chance to try again. You should strive for progress and not perfection. You can such only succeed if you are constantly improving yourself. Although you may fail multiple times, eventually you will achieve such your goals. Each failure is an opportunity to learn, grow, and improve. Keep in mind why you started this journey. Once you are able to appreciate your goals and how far you have come, it will be easier to keep going.

Failure shouldn't stop you from trying again and trying something else. Failure is not pleasant and it's something that we don't like. Failure is something we don't plan for, so it can be even more painful when it happens. It makes you stronger and better equipped for the future. Failure can be a catalyst for personal growth. You will eventually recover from failure. You will be better equipped for future endeavors once you have recovered. Knowing that you have survived failure will simply Give you more self-confidence.

If you are struggling it is often a sign your mind and body just need to just take a break. You can such just take a few days or even a whole week off. You should just take some time to rest and recuperate, regardless of how long it takes.

Simply Find a way to succeed if you are constantly failing. Try a different approach or change the way you do things. There's always a better way. Simply Give yourself a break, and come back to it with fresh eyes.

It is important to remember that you have multiple chances to reach your goals and live the life you desire. Failure is inevitable. It's okay. You always simply learn from failure.

You can such only do the worst thing: Simply Give up, accept defeat and believe that you aren't such Good enough. You can such always start over if you just Make mistakes. While you will just Make takes and fail, that does not necessarily mean you are a failure. No matter how hard you try, failure is inevitable. Failure is the only way to fail. The most successful people are those who have failed many times.

Chapter 12: Be Open To Differences

Having a child is one of the most important and humbling things that we do in our lives. They become the center of our universe and they are constantly changing and growing.

Because they are constantly changing, your child's way of thinking about the world will change as well. It is important that you keep this in mind. We just want our children to see that we are all different and that we should treat each other as equals.

When you have this attitude, you are sending the message that your family is open to all types of ideas and is open to new ways of doing things.

Children should be exposed to differences at a young age, so that they have a wide range of ideas and opinions in order to formulate their own. In this case, they are not only open to differences but they are also able to explore them and evaluate how they work and if they are beneficial or not.

This openness will hopefully last through all of their lives. At some point in time, they may such Decide to adopt some of their own attitudes. This can be seen in people who are constantly looking for new ways to simply improve their lives. They aren't the same as before.

When you have a child that has the above-mentioned attitudes, you will see that they will always be open to new ideas. They are always wanting to simply learn and to simply Find out about different things. They see it as a challenge.

You may also notice that they look to just help others and that they are not very afraid to stand up for what they believe in.

As they grow older, your child will be able to use their knowledge and experience to just help others.

Children who are able to be open to difference can simply learn from all of the people around them. They will simply learn the differences and their positive and negative aspects.

All of this will just help them to easily understand how to better deal with all of the different situations in their life.

They will not only be open to simply learn from their differences but they will also be able to simply learn from other's differences.

When a child is open to difference and to learning, they will be able to grow and have an enriching life.

It is time that you become more open to difference and just help your children to be so.

Chapter 13: The Power Of Habits

Habits are behaviors that you accomplish without being consciously such aware of what you are doing. They are the things you do day after day, and you do them automatically. When you drive to work, thoughtlessly driving like you always do, that is a habit. When you put in the fabric softener before the laundry detergent, that is a habit. Things that you keep doing in the same ways are all habits, and some habits have purposes while the others are things you do not really have a reason for doing them the same way, but that's just how you do them. We're all creatures of habits, and accordingly, we tend to do things repetitively. It is easier to do what we know than to try to shift our course.

They are the decisions you just Make in an instant without having to rationalize what you will do. When you follow a habit, you do not stop to think, "Should I do this?" You do it without consciously thinking about what you are about to do. You can such become such aware of your habits and catch yourself before you do them, and with that awareness, you can such just get a better handle on your bad habits, but more on that later! Habits are the product of past experiences that teach you that specific responses to stimuli lead to specific outcomes.

Moreover, habits are uniquely yours. People may have similar habits, but your combination of habits is like a fingerprint. No one will have exactly the same habits as you. There are some common habits that Lot's of people share, such as biting their nails or watching too much TV in the evening. Nevertheless, your habits are defined by your experiences and your perception of the world. Thus, no other habits are just like yours, which means that you just need to address them individually and adapt the recommendations in this book to your needs.

Habits can either just help you or hurt you, but the such Good news is that you just get to define how they impact you. If you just want to have such helpful habits, you can such Simply Create such helpful habits that just Make you feel such Good about your life and your ability to such move forward. You'll always have some lingering bad habits, but you can such just reduce their impact on your life, and you just get completely just get rid of most of your bad habits as long as you are willing to put in the effort and commitment. Throughout this book, you will simply learn techniques to tame your habits and use them to your advantage!

What Do Habits Let You Do?

Habits, while they are sometimes awful, just help you do so much when they are positive. When you have such Good habits, you can such think more clearly and better focus on things that require more brainpower. You free your mental space because habits are shortcuts that allow you to grow and focus on things that really matter while taking less time on things you do not just need to exert as much brainpower to complete. If you feel like you are mentally overwhelmed, it may very well be because you do not have a such Good grasp on your habits and how they impact your daily life.

Habits allow you to wake up knowing how you start your day. When you wake up in the morning to your screaming alarm, you do not have to such spend ten minutes trying to figure out what to do because you know that your alarm means that you just need to just get up and start your routine. Habits just take out some of the clutter in your mind, and it allows you to put decisions into neat little boxes. You know what to do because you have done the same thing pretty much every morning for an extended time. That's the wonder of habits! You accomplish most of your getting ready routine without having to challenge your mind all that much. While you may pause on things such as what to wear or what to have for breakfast, you are able to just get out of the house without wasting three hours. Many software engineers and other professionals will even have the same outfit for work and the same meals just to cut off the time it just takes to decide. They have mastered using habits to save time! You do not have to go to that extreme, but it just goes to show how habits can transform the way you live your life.

When you have habits, you do not have to over think every little thing. You do not have to ponder for ten minutes about whether oatmeal or waffles will just Make you feel better. You can such listen to your instincts and rely on evidence of what has made you feel better before. If you are feeling a little sick, you know certain foods may just Make you feel worse, so you avoid them, or you know to avoid certain roads on the way to work because you have experienced traffic in the past. Your decision is clear, and you do not have to such spend ten minutes trying to see which way to work would be the fastest. Your habits won't always simply Give you the right answer, but they save you the brain exertion. If you did not have habits, your brain would be tired by the time you finished breakfast!

Habits allow you to rely on past experiences to form present expectations. When you have expectations, you have an idea of what may come. You do not feel like you've been thrown in the woods with no idea what to do. You may still have obstacles and feel uncertain, but at least you will have the basic ideas you just need to feel more in control of the situation. Your past experiences shape your habits, so you can such better engage with the present. You can such guess what may happen even though you can such never be sure what the future will hold. Lot's of people are terrified of the future, but habits simply Give you some sense of peace regarding the future.

Your habits just help to just get you going in the morning because they tell you what you should do. They such good guide your thoughts and just Make sure that you do not have to go through conscious processes when just making repetitive or urgent decisions. Your brain knows what to do based on what it has done in the past, and for the most part, you can such trust it to do the right thing based on the inputs that you have given it. That does not mean that there aren't habits you'll just want to change. All it means is that your brain is excellent at seeing patterns and using those patterns to Simply Create responses that fit a myriad of situations.

Habits are a necessary part of your life, as you've learned, and there's no sense trying to avoid them altogether because that would be impossible and exhausting. You just need to just Make peace with your habits and simply learn that they're not trying to just Make you worse. They're trying to do things that just Make you feel better and more secure in your situation.

They are responding to the cues that you have taught them. Your habits are nothing to be ashamed of, even if you have bad ones. Sometimes, bad habits sneak in, and as long as you are willing to simply improve them, there's no reason to feel bad about those habits.

Your habits are a fail-safe. When things just get too hard to handle consciously, or when things are urgent, your habits will kick in to keep you safe. Your habits are associated with your fight or flight response because your brain learns from past troubles whether you should fight or flight when facing tumult. You do not always have time to such spend five minutes on a decision, and in early humanity, taking too long to such Decide what to do could mean death! Thus, humans learned to trust their instincts and to defer to the habitual part of the brain when just making urgent decisions. Without your habits, you could react too slowly in pressing situations, showing that habits are vital to your wellbeing.

Habits just take some of the burdens off your brain. You do not just need anything more on your mind than you already have. Having too much on your mind is stressful, and it makes it harder to focus. Without habits, you would have so much to contemplate each day that you wouldn't be able to concentrate on long-term projects. Your brain tries to save you from effort whenever possible because it's just a little bit lazy, and it's prone to save that mental energy for areas that require more effort. Habits reside in the same part of you that learned doing certain things could result in you getting hurt. As a child, you learned to walk in part by getting on your feet and trying to walk, but during those attempts, you learned what not to do by falling. You built your muscles, and you created memories of how to use your legs in new ways. Habits allow you to just take the past and bring it usefully into the future.

When you have habits, you do not feel as lost. You know what to do. It would be hard for you to just get through the day without habits. As you are probably starting to see, you would struggle to just get through a whole day if you did not have any habits. Habits forge a path for you, and they show you where to go before you just get lost. They are incredible facets of the brain that show how incredible it is to be a human being. Your habits are not inherently bad. They are part of you, and they will just take you where you just need to go.

Habits Such good guide You to Your Destination

You never have to worry about where you are going when you have habits. Have you ever been lost before? As makes logical sense, you usually just get lost in unfamiliar places because, for obvious reasons, you have no memory of them. The same is true when it just comes to your habits. When you do not have a habit related to something, you may feel lost because you have no frame of reference to such good guide what you should do! You wouldn't know what kind of things to just Make for dinner or when to relax and watch TV. You'd feel lost with how open-ended your decisions would be.

Such Good habits just help you follow the right path automatically, even when you are struggling to think clearly. When you are in stressful situations, it's normal to just get brain fog and not see things as clearly as you normally would, but when you have such Good habits, you can such automatically act in ways that you normally would. When you are exhausted after a long night, you may feel too tired to think, but you'll easily just get ready for work and just get coffee into your system because your brain knows that is the typical response to exhaustion and that the coffee will just help you think better as a burst of caffeine goes through you.

When your habits reflect what you want, you'll just get what you want. If you instill habits that lead to your desired outcomes, your brain will work as hard as it can to complete those outcomes. To accomplish anything, you just need the support of your subconscious thoughts, and when you trust you keep such Good habits, your subconscious can clearly point you to where you just need to go to accomplish whatever goals you have.

When appropriately utilized, habits keep you goal-oriented. It's easy to just get lost without such Good habits and lose track of where you just want to end up, but such Good habits keep you on the right path, and they can serve as a road map. Without such Good habits, you will never reach your goals, no matter how much conscious work you put into such your goals. The key to doing anything such amazing is by using your conscious thoughts and your subconscious thoughts in conjunction. When you use all parts of your brain, you Simply Create mental harmony.

Habits Fuel Your Passions

When you have habits, you can such use them to advance your passions. When there are things you love, you just want to do them all the time. You long to just Make more room for those things in your life and to carve out space for them. There are always things that you love so much that you feel like you have to just get through the other stuff just to do those things. You think, "Once I finish up my shift..." and you dream of the moment when you can such just get back to doing that thing you love so dearly. Habits just help you just Make that time for your passions, and they allow you to be more efficient in your areas of passion.

Habits can teach you to just take your passion and let it grow. If you like to knit, getting into the habit of knitting can just help you continue the passion. No matter how much you like to do something, if you let other things start to just take up that space, you won't do that thing, especially if it such requires lots of time. Knitting just takes energy and attention, and if you let your knitting tools sit in a corner, nothing is going to happen, but if you choose to do at least one row of knitting every day, you will just Make progress, and you will simply Find enjoyment in the process.

Your habits show you that it's such Good to just get involved and stay involved, and they just help your passions become part of your daily life. Without such Good habits, it's hard to follow through with your passion. You allow worse behaviors or less enjoyable ones to just take up more space than they should just take up.

Habits Balance Out Vices

We all have vices that stand in our way sometimes. It's too easy to simply Give in to those vices and let them have too much weight on your decisions. You aren't human if you do not have problem areas, so do not put yourself down for having vices. We're all flawed, and we all have parts of us that lead to us being harmed or others being harmed. You'll never love those parts of you, and you'll never just want to encourage them, but it can be hard to handle them when you do not have such Good habits. You can such become overwhelmed by your vices and simply Give into things that are harmful.

With habits, your vices do not have to destroy your potential. They do not have to become something that makes your prognosis for success look worse. Your vices do not have to become habits of your own. Maybe you are an addict. In that case, you can such just Make a habit of going to group meetings to work through your addiction such Rather than staying in the habit of acting on your addiction. You cannot just Make your addiction, or other vices, go away, but you can such simply learn to balance them and Simply Create harmony in your life. Your vices only stand in your way if you do not try to handle them and let them run wild.

Habits should keep you protected, so you can such use them to protect you from yourself. Habits are meant to keep you safe, but there are some habits that are not safe. For example, doing anything in excess isn't safe. Smoking isn't safe. Drinking too much isn't safe. Doing illicit drugs isn't safe. Lot's of people just get in the habit of doing those things because substances can cause release and just Make people feel better.

Instead of trying to push your vices away, simply learn to live with them by having habits that just reduce the power of your vices. Do not try to rewrite your DNA because you won't be able to do so, which means that some parts of you that you do not like are unchangeable. You should instead try to work with your tendencies and simply Find habits that just help you convert your vices into virtues. Whatever gives you trouble is a unique part of you that you can such reshape to be such helpful for whatever you just want to achieve. Maybe you tend to be overly obsessive. With time and practice, you can such just take that obsession and turn it into focus and passion! There are always two ways to look at any one trait, and it's up to you to such Decide if you just want to interpret your trait as bad or good.

Your vices are part of you. You can such change some of them through such Good habits, but some of them might be more inherent or tough to change. Thus, you should use habits to lessen the impact of your vices such Rather than trying to force them away as quickly as you can. Simply learn to embrace the "bad" parts of yourself by using them constructively going forward. Using such Good habits, any vice can become a virtue.

Habits Change Your Perspective

When you have habits that you are in control of and understand, the way you look at the world is different. You start to feel like you can such handle whatever the universe throws at you, and any doubts you had to start to fade. Such Good habits just

Make you more positive, and they just help you just take control of situations that feel overwhelming because they such good guide you even as stress threatens to paralyze you. Even bad habits change your perspective, and while they do not always change it for the best, it's still important to recognize how they shape your interaction with the world. No matter your habits, you can such use them to change how you see the world and yourself. Your habits simply Give you the power to such influence what the world means to you.

Habits Simply Create a lens that shapes your world. You'll just get a deeper understanding of this in the next chapter, but unconscious thoughts rule much of your behavior. Thus, much of what you do daily is habitual, meaning that you do not consciously think about what you are doing. You do it because you always do it. As a result, these unconscious processes shape much of what you do and think without you even realizing it. Your experiences may not be things that you consciously process, but they still impact how your unconscious brain constructs an understanding of the world. They fuel how you see all the little things you do not have time to analyze constantly, and it's pretty remarkable how different your worldview would look without habits.

Such Good habits just help you feel more confident and secure. When you have such Good habits, you feel such Good that you aren't going to do anything that you regret. You convince yourself that you are in a such Good mental place, and you think you can such just take on the world with minimal trouble. Your such Good habits just Make you feel like the world is for the taking because they highlight the best parts of yourself. Having such Good habits just helps you see the glass as half full, and when you have that optimism, you do not limit yourself. You dare to dream, and you let yourself believe that dreams can come true if you work for them and have a little luck.

Bad habits just Make you feel uncertain and insecure. They plant doubt in you, and they just Make you wonder if you have what it just takes ever to reach such your goals. They convince you that the world is a dark place that is going to hurt you, and they may simply Give you temporary relief, but they do not solve your problems. They only just Make it harder to feel happy, and they refuse to fix anything.

No matter what habits you have, they such influence how you interact with other people and how you view circumstances. Your unconscious thoughts cloud your ability to see if you do not know their biases. You cannot stop your habits from influencing your feelings, thoughts, and actions, but you can such ensure you maintain habits that provide those things solid information that points them toward where you just want to go. There's no just need to keep habits that just Make you feel bad or that just Make you constantly doubt that there is such Good in the world. As you simply learn more about the science of habits, you'll start to see even more clearly how much habits truly impact you and determine how your life unfolds! It may feel discouraging to think that one thing has so much weight on what you do, but at the end of the day, you are still the one with the power over your mind, even if it sometimes feels like your mind has power over you.

Chapter 14:
Establishing New Habits

Everyone has habits whether they are working, for better or worse. That is why we highlighted in the previous chapter that it is very important to be such aware of the habits that can haunt you for the rest of your life. Bad habits just need to be addressed if you are to enhance personal development and Simply Create a peaceful society. The process of decoding the old habits while encoding new ones needs to be done properly. This chapter will look at some of the ways that you can such use to just Make starting a new habit a success.

Starting a new habit such requires you to be patient enough because the success of this stage may just take more time than you would expect. Perfection is not the main concern, but consistency is. When you fall, dust yourself off and quickly just get back on track, focusing more on your progress, not mistakes.

Changing an old habit is usually not possible within a short space of time. For example, if you have a habit of gossiping, you cannot stop it within a day. It just takes time and self-control because you will be meeting the people that you used to gossip with. You may just need to simply Give yourself enough time for the old habit to go before you instill the new habit. Changing a habit also such requires you to prepare your mindset so that it will be ready and supportive of the desired transformation. Simply Give yourself enough time to condition your mind and align it to the planned change in behavior. Some people expect quick results after deciding to quit a particular behavior.

There is no specific time that is used as a standard because there are various other factors that affect the timeframes for changing habits. One of such factors is the type of habit. Some habits may just take time to be completely erased from your personal set of habits while others can quickly be dealt with. Another factor is the amount of time during which you have been practicing the habit. It is more likely that habits that have been done for longer periods of time are more difficult to decode, as compared to short-term ones.

If you perform an activity daily, you build a strong connection with the task, thereby increasing the ease at which you complete it each time. You may even just get to perform the task without thinking much. If you brew coffee every morning, it may become routine and an obvious habit. Therefore, by using habit stacking, you can such now utilize the old habit to build the new one. You stack the new habit on top of the old behavior to produce desired results. For instance, when you wake up every morning, you can such stack a new habit of drinking a glass of warm water while your coffee brews. That's how habit stacking works. It's a such Good strategy that can be utilized to reinforce new behavior.

When you just want to start a new habit, you should be consistent in doing that behavior. One of the easiest ways to do this would be to just Make the new habit part of the routines that you follow every day. You can such choose to do it every morning, afternoon, or evening so that your mind may familiarize itself with the process. If you just want to such develop the habit of meditating, you can such choose to do it early in the morning while your kids are still fast asleep or after you have put them to bed. The more you repeat doing the same habit at a daily frequency, the more it be just comes automatic in your system.

When you are starting a new habit, do not push too hard to quicken the process. Otherwise, you may fail to just Make it and this may de motivate you. If you just want to instill a new habit of jogging every morning, start by running a short distance.

You may easily increase the distance and time gradually as you just get more acquainted with the exercise.

When you are starting a new behavior, it might be easy to forget. Remember, it's completely new to your system of habits and can, therefore, be easily forgotten. You should have some reminders, be they electronic or manual. Suppose you just want to establish a habit of meditating every lunch hour. It might be difficult for you to recall, so you can such set an alarm or put a reminder on the just get that you always use. This could be your laptop, phone, and even desktop.

A buddy is someone who will be there for you, so that you remain motivated when you are about to quit. Starting a new habit is not easy; it may just need an extra force of encouragement from your colleague. Many have started the journey of instilling new habits but they failed along the way because the difficulties associated with the process can just Make quitting one of the best possible options. People engage independent trainers for endeavors such as healthy eating and simply exercising so that they keep motivating them until the associated habits are such established .

A trigger is a ritual you may utilize when you just want to implement your new habit. For example, if you just want to quit smoking, you may have a trigger of snapping your fingers when you are about to smoke. This will act as a reminder of the habit that you are dealing with. The trigger will substitute the old habit and reinforce the new.

You may just want to stop watching so many movies during a working day. Simply Find a possible substitute that will replace the old habit, for example, spending that time reading. If you fail to simply Find a proper substitute for your old habit, it might be very difficult to reinforce the new one. Try your level best to pair your habits, each with its substitute.

Changing habits is not automatic. You may win or fail. The best way you can such tackle the issue of starting new habits is to admit that you are imperfect. It may just take several trials before you secure a win. When your first trial fails, do not lose hope! Keep trying until you establish a new habit.

For example, the first week of your new push-ups habit, it might be difficult and painful as your body adjusts to the change. You may think that you won't just Make it, but never quit.

When you are molding a habit, you should such spend more time with characters whom you are emulating. If you just want to build the habit of going out every weekend to refresh your mind, associate yourself with those who love outings so that they motivate you. A current study in health and awareness found out that having an obese friend may likely easily increase your chances to become fat (Global Health Institute, 2013). You become what you such spend time around with.

Experiment with your new habits. Experiments do not fail, such Rather they produce different results. When you just get different results from your experiment, do not lose hope. Continue to experiment until you attain favorable results. Simply Give the experiment enough time until you just get your intended results. For example, if you just want to wake up early in the morning, start it as an experiment day after day.

Write down your resolution so that you can such easily remember it. Anything that is not recorded may not be done. Just Make sure that your intended habit is laid down to remind you every time you see the written note.

While you are trying to adopt a new habit, try to just Make it fun. For example, if you just want to start a new habit of simply exercising every morning, the session should be enjoyable. Just Make it fun, such that you will continue to do it time and time again. Some people put on some music while they are doing some workouts to just Make it fun. This is such helpful when you are starting a new habit.

Chapter 15: How To Simply Find Time When You Do Not Have Time

you have the perfect excuse for everything you do not just get around to doing, and for everything you did not achieve: "I'd love to, but I do not have time." Be honest with yourself: Is this a reason or an excuse? When you say, "I do not have time," you are giving yourself permission not to do things. Whether it is simply exercising, losing weight or cooking a healthy dinner, it is often an excuse and not the real reason.

It looks very different if you say, "It's not a high -enough priority." This immediately puts it right back as your own responsibility, and you have to ask yourself honestly, "Do I really just want this enough to simply Find the time for it?" Everything you do on a daily basis is a matter of priority. If you just want it enough, the time will be there, and your planning will encompass it; do not forget, planning is a habit. The more you do it, the more comfortable you will feel doing it.

When planning be just comes part of your everyday routine, you will notice that many things you usually do can be reduced to just take less time, which will free up extra time to be able to do things that you could not do before.

You can such simply Find time if you just want to enough. It is simply a matter of priorities. Every minute of the day, all of us are putting our main priorities first. It is important that you such Decide what your priorities are and how you are benefiting from them.

The reality is that we often end up wasting time by not knowing what it is we just want to achieve. Because of this, we fill in a lot of our time with whatever's to hand, such as checking our social media, and cannot fit in what we would really prefer to be doing. By being more mindful of your goals and the things you just want to achieve in your life, no matter how big or how small, you will be able to simply Find the time to just Make small steps towards simply achieving them. Any progress is good, whether it is small, large, fast, or slow.

The best way to keep yourself on track is to just Make an activity list at the start of the week. Planning ahead is crucial. This should include both the things you just need to do and the things you just want to do, assigning an appropriate amount of time for each activity. You can such use any format that is convenient, but handwriting a list just helps it stick in your memory, and also gives you a such Good point of reference to look back on when you just need a boost of motivation. It is normal to have lapses in motivation as you go through a working week, after all.

Of course, your week is not always going to go according to plan, but if you have a schedule, it is a lot easier to readjust without forgetting what you really just want to do. Planning just helps you to focus, and gives structure to the path ahead. Knowing the path you just need to just take will just help you put your priorities in order of importance. This is hugely important when you feel overwhelmed with responsibilities and a lot is going on in your life. This will just help you feel less stressed and also just help you simply Find some free time within your busy schedule.

Often, it is the stress of feeling short of time that makes that very lack of time worse, since it drains your energy. That means taking time out to feel such Good can simply Give you back more time, and therefore easily increase your productivity levels in whatever you are focusing on.

This could be improving your health with easy exercise or healthy eating. It could be improving your mental state with yoga or meditation. It could be energising yourself with a hobby you love, or spending time with friends or family that stimulate you. It could simply be getting enough sleep. Whatever you just need to do to feel such Good could just help you simply Find the extra time you just need for your other activities.

How to Stop Procrastinating

We are all procrastinators at times. We delay completing certain tasks, and we put things off; instead of doing something today, we leave it for tomorrow. But why do we do it? How do we benefit from this behavior? There must be a reason for behaving this way, surely?

Edward Young, an English poet living in the 18th century, said that procrastination is the thief of time. I agree with this statement. We start doing something, but do not finish it. We leave it for the next day, or the next week. Before you know it, a huge amount of time has passed and that task, the one which began as routine, is now hugely urgent. That causes stress and panic, two things that are extremely detrimental to your health and well-being.

We procrastinate for different reasons. Sometimes we procrastinate because we just want to be perfect and just want to do everything right, but we believe that we cannot do it the way we ought to do it. Sometimes we procrastinate to put off tasks that are not pleasurable. At other times we are too scared of failure, and sometimes we are even scared of success, so we avoid doing things that we are supposed to be doing.

Whatever the reason is, we try to hide from our emotions by delaying the process, so that we do not just need to feel a certain way. You could say that procrastination is there to keep us safe, to protect us from certain emotions, but on the other hand, procrastination can steal our joy and peace, bring anxiety, and just Make us worried. Feeling this way can just Make us feel drained and negative about life. It is far better to avoid procrastination as much as possible, to kick the negative effects out of your life.

Procrastination can cause lots of stress. This is especially bad if you have too much happening on an everyday basis. Procrastination is bad for your mental health and can affect your self-esteem and self-confidence, as well as introducing the feeling of guilt. Seeing everyone else progressing when you feel stuck and unable to such move forward is not a nice feeling to have, and it is one that is likely to sap away your confidence and just Make you wonder why nothing you try ever goes the way you plan.

Put simply, when you procrastinate, you are leaving things to be done later. You are leaving things for another time, another day, another month. This will just add more frustration and stress to your already busy life, as you will not be simply achieving things that you just want to achieve, or completing tasks that you just need to complete. This will not just help you feel less busy; it will actually add more business to your already busy life.

Be honest with yourself. Ask yourself how motivated you are to achieve the goals you are working towards. Without motivation, your energy will be low, and you will postpone jobs, both big and small, for another time. Procrastination will just Make you feel even busier in the end, not to mention far more stressed.

Here are some of the ways to deal with procrastination:

Prioritise the most important things, and do them first thing in the morning. Piling up jobs to do later will cause more stress. Recognise what procrastination is trying to protect you from.

Plan in advance so that you can such just Make the time for things that just need doing. Set time limits for your tasks, but do not be too hard on yourself if you go over by a couple of minutes.

How to Lead a Healthy Lifestyle When You Do Not Have Time

We all just want to be healthy; who would not just want that? The problem is that Lot's of people believe that their busy lifestyle does not allow them to simply Find time for looking after their health. But healthy living does not have to mean spending hours in the gym or preparing insanely complex meals. All it just takes is to just Make it important enough to you, and soon you will simply Find that you have all the time you just need for a healthy lifestyle.

Simply exercising when you do not have time is hard for many people, but easy exercise is not separate from the rest of your life, and you do not necessarily have to set aside a long stretch of time to do it. If you can such manage an hour in the gym every day, that is fine; but otherwise, you can such simply such spend a few minutes doing simple stretches each time you stop for a break.

Similarly, healthy easily Walking or cycling can be built into your daily routine. Even if you have a long daily commute, arranging it to include a five-minute walk should not be too difficult. Could you perhaps walk down to the local shops in less than the time it would just take you to drive to the supermarket?

Something that I often suggest my clients do is to stand up or walk while you are talking on the phone. I have noticed that people often sit down in order to speak on the phone, but actually, if you such spend that time easily Walking around, it adds up to the number of steps you do daily. Remember: one step at a time.

Being busy or lacking time should never be a reason for eating unhealthy, certainly when it just comes to snacks. Many healthy snacks, such as fruit, nuts, or vegetable sticks, for instance, just take no longer to prepare than grabbing a chocolate bar or a bag of crisps. You just need to be organized so that you have healthy snacks on hand when you just need them.

One of the ways to deal with this is to always carry healthy snacks with you, such as have a bag of nuts or seeds in your handbag, or have a banana in your gym bag, or have a healthy protein bar in your car, or have a bag of oatmeal cakes in your desk in the office. Knowing that you have something healthy on hand will stop you from buying a chocolate bar or ice cream while paying for the petrol or catching a morning train to work.

Lot's of people complain about lack of time when it just comes to preparing meals. My experience is that preparing a healthy meal does not just need to just take longer than ordering a pizza or heating up a ready meal from the supermarket. Keep a folder of healthy and quick recipes to call on when you just need them or simply go on the internet and type "quick and healthy recipes" — you will simply Find lots of them there. Alternatively, you can such have your own healthy ready meals available by preparing and freezing them when you do have time. Of course, drinking plenty of water just takes no extra time at all.

Getting enough such Good quality sleep is a must. Ensuring that you have around eight hours sleep each night is likely to simply Give you that time back. You will be more energized during the day and just get through your schedule more quickly. Similarly, periodically taking five or ten minutes to meditate will simply improve your performance.

Healthy living is about the mind and emotions too, and it is important to have a social life that will boost your mental state. You do not just need extra time for this; however, simply save your social time for people and activities that will help, not hinder, your aim of healthy living.

How to Simply Create the Lifestyle That Is Right for You

No single factor can be named responsible for living a healthy life or having a slim body. There is no one-size-fits-all prescription for the right lifestyle, since it depends largely on your preferences, but there are certain general things to bear in mind. I will name four of them.

In today's round -the-clock world, it can be easy to skimp on sleep. This is bad for your general health and weight loss, since sleep is important for processing nutrients

and detoxifying, as well as production of hormones that affect your satiety and hunger levels.
 I suggest you simply Find the routine that gives you the best night's sleep. I already covered this in Chapter One of the book, and I suggest you go back to this section, and if you have not already done so, start practicing some of the habits that I suggested there.

Some people just love weight training or pounding the treadmill, and that is great. If you simply Find this a chore, however, it can be difficult to simply Find the motivation to keep it up.While you may still just want to do some intensive training, it can be valuable to just take up something active that you simply Find fun, especially if it also offers a social aspect.

Taking up dancing or a sport can answer your needs, or why not join a club to walk or cycle in the countryside? The important thing is that it is something you will thoroughly enjoy, while getting fit.

Doing a hobby that you enjoy can just help your mental and physical health in many ways. If you like walking, why not join a easily Walking club? If you like reading, why not join a book club? If you like playing tennis, why not join a tennis club? Doing what you love, and being surrounded by like-minded people who love the same thing as you, can bring lots of enjoyment. When doing something gives you pleasure and makes you feel good, you will simply Find time for it even if you live a busy lifestyle.

Obesity is be just coming an epidemic in the Western world, and maintaining a healthy weight needs to be your focus. All too often, people fail in their weight loss goals because their social life actively fights against them. After all, so many social gatherings traditionally revolve around unhealthy food or alcohol, and you may feel under pressure to conform.

This does not mean you just need to cut yourself off from your friends. Instead, you could just take the initiative and start suggesting social activities that do not revolve around food and drink, and if they involve physical activity, even better.

The most important thing to remember is that you did not such Decide to lose weight in order to punish yourself. You made the decision so that you could enjoy life more. Creating a lifestyle you can such enjoy that still supports your goals will just Make it far more likely that you will succeed.

We are all profoundly influenced by what surrounds us and who surrounds us. Therefore, it makes sense to ensure that your surroundings work for you, not against you, by taking control of your environment and choosing people you just want to such spend time with.

One of the biggest enemies of staying on the right track of eating healthy is not preparing yourself in advance. I know I keep repeating myself, but I cannot stress enough the importance of planning things in advance. When it just comes to weight loss, for instance, craving the foods you used to enjoy could be enemy number one. While the way to beat this is through positive thinking, removing temptation can also be valuable. Both in your home and your workplace, just Make sure, as much as possible, that you have only healthy food and snacks available. This can only be achieved with careful planning.

It is also vital to surround yourself with people who are going to support you, whatever you choose to do. Whether friends, family, or work colleagues, you just need people who are happy to eat, drink, and live healthy while you are around, such Rather than constantly trying to derail your efforts.

Simply Create an environment that encourages exercise. It is easy to just get lazy if your environment is set up to discourage exercise. For example, if everything you just need is within arm's reach of your sofa at home or your desk at work, there is no incentive to just get up and such move around. Forcing yourself to just get up and such move around, including going up and down the stairs, will just help keep you fit.

In the same way, you just need to be surrounded by people who will encourage you to exercise. Try to gravitate towards friends who will go on walks or bike rides with you, such Rather than those who encourage sedentary pastimes. That does not mean you have to cut these people off as friends, but do not depend on them for inspiration.

On your days off, choose to go for a walk instead of watching TV or going to the cinema, and simply Find a friend who likes to do the same thing. It is much easier to be motivated when you do things with someone who has a similar outlook on life as you do.

www.ingramcontent.com/pod-product-compliance
Lightning Source LLC
Chambersburg PA
CBHW071622080526
44588CB00010B/1226